The Chessboard

and Other Story-Object Lessons.

BY EDITH MORRISON

ILKESTON,

Moorley's Bible & Bookshop Ltd.

1974

ISBN 0 901495 50 6

<u>F O R E W O R D</u>

<u>BY REV. SAMUEL WORKMAN.</u>

44 Dillons Avenue,
Whiteabbey,
Newtownabbey,
Co. Antrim,
N.Ireland.

Dear Reader,

The "Story-Object Lessons" which are contained in this book were first written for my personal use.

During Sunday morning service, my congregation includes several hundred children and I devote a short time to speaking to them each week. As the years passed it became increasingly difficult to obtain original and suitable material, of an evangelistic nature to meet their needs. I therefore requested the author, a lady who has had many years of experience in child evangelism, to help me in my search for children's stories. She responded by writing this volume of "Story Object Lessons".

For some years her work has been of great value to my Church, not only to the children, but even to their parents. It is my hope and belief that these stories should now be published for the benefit of all Christian ministers and workers who pray that the boys and girls in their charge may be led to know Christ as Saviour and Lord.

I am,

Yours faithfully,

<u>Samuel Workman.</u>

CONTENTS

(HOLD UP CHESSBOARD WRAPPED IN PAPER).

I have with me here an object used in a game. It begins with C. I wonder if any of you can guess what it is? (ACCEPT A FEW SUGGESTIONS THEN UNWRAP PARCEL. SHOW GAME OF CHESS TO THE CHILDREN).

One day Billy's Daddy came home and handed him a game of chess. "There's nothing like playing chess to make you smart, my lad," he smiled. After that the two of them often had an exciting game together. As the weeks passed by, however, Billy didn't want to play so often. He spent more and more time with his pals and Daddy didn't mind that of course. It's a good thing for young people to play with those of their own age. No, it was something else which worried his father; Billy was always getting into trouble. One day he played football near the greenhouse and broke a window. That was bad enough because Daddy had told him not to play <u>near</u> the greenhouse. There were plenty of other places where he could have played, not only that, but Billy said that he had not broken it and put the blame on one of his friends.

Daddy tried to help Billy to see how wrong
he had been.   "Listen Billy! First, you were
disobedient and disobedience is a sin because God
has said that children are to obey their parents.
Then you told a lie, which you know I hate, but
what is more important, God hates lies.   Last of
all you put the blame on a friend which was not
only deceitful but cruel and disloyal." Billy
didn't seem in the least bit worried. "I'm sorry
Dad.   Of course I'm sorry, but you make such a
fuss about it, anyone would think I had committed
<u>murder</u>. After all, being disobedient and telling
a few fibs are only <u>small</u> sins." At first Daddy
was at a loss to make the little boy see how much
his wrong doing mattered,   then he had a brain-
wave!   "Billy", he asked, "Bring me your chessboard".   "Good", said Billy, as he opened it out
on the table. "Let's have a nice game and forget
all about sins and things".

(SPREAD OUT THE BOARD FOR CHILDREN TO SEE).

"Instead of playing a game," said Daddy, "I want
to tell you a story about a king who played chess
only you will need a long piece of paper and a
pencil."   Feeling mystified, Billy found these.
"Once upon a time there lived an eastern king who
loved to play chess.   This king had an enemy who
was always making war on him. One day he discovered that this enemy also liked playing chess, so
the king thought of a crafty plan to outwit his
enemy and ruin him.   He pretended to make peace
with him and then invited him to the palace to
play chess.   After they had finished, his old
enemy said, "Thank you very much for your invit-
ation, I have never enjoyed a game so well...es-
pecially as I won.   I would like to reward your
kindness in some way."   The crafty king replied,
"Just one small favour I beg of you."   "Certainly," replied the other.   "Tell me what it is."
Lifting up the chessboard the king said, "Behold

the number of squares on this board all I ask is
one grain of wheat for the first square,   two
grains for the second, four for the next, sixteen
for the next and so on..."   (POINT AS YOU SPEAK).

"Is that all you ask?" replied his old enemy.
"Such a small request, I promise to send you the
wheat or the price of the wheat on my return
home."

        Soon he was home again and he sat down with
paper and pencil to work out the amount.   "Let's
see," he began.   "This won't take long...one for
the first square...two for the second...four for
the third...sixteen for the fourth...ah...it's a
bit harder now...let me see, what do I have to do
...multiply the answer each time by itself.   Now
sixteen by sixteen...O dear...this is going to
take longer than I thought. I'd better give this
to one of my wise men to work out, the only thing
I'm good at is fighting, I'm afraid I'm not much
use at sums."

        One of the wise men did as the king request-
ed.   It took him a very long time and when at
last he came before the king his face was deathly
white. "Your Majesty, you are ruined. All   the
wheat fields in the country would never yield
what you owe, to pay your debt, it will take
everything you possess."   Only then did the King
realise he had been tricked, he had been stripped
of everything!

        When Daddy had finished he said to Billy,
"Now <u>you try to</u> work out how much he owed." Billy
liked sums.   He worked on his problem for the
rest of the evening.   "I can't go on any longer
I've nowhere near finished and already it's running into millions," he yawned sleepily.   "I told
you that story tonight," said Daddy, "because I
want to show you that you also have an enemy. His
name is Satan.   He works very much like the

crafty king in the story.   First of all he asks
you for very little...what you call 'small' sins,
then very, very quickly these sins multiply, until they affect every part of your life.   In the
end you will find that Satan has stripped you of
everything, - your best friends, your good name,
your character, your health, your peace of mind,
your happiness,   your position and in the end
your very soul."

        Billy was silent.   He knew only too well
that his father was speaking the truth.   He
thought of his disobedience, his lies, his un-
kindness, and lots of other things his father
didn't know about.   "You're right Daddy," said
Billy slowly.   "But I <u>do</u> want to stop before it
is too late, I'll do what you have asked me to do
so often, I'll turn away from doing these things.
I know that Jesus had to suffer the punishment
for all those rotten things I've done. I'll give
Him the rest of my life.   I'll ask Him into my
heart right now."

        Boys and girls I do beg of you to do this
same thing.....before Satan has robbed you of
everything just like the wiley king robbed his
enemy. Be more than a match for Satan, hand over
your life to Jesus right now.....as we shut our
eyes.

THE GOLDEN TOUCH

OBJECTS NEEDED......1. Any gold coloured objects...belts, watches, ornaments, etc.

2. Sketch or picture of the sun (or point to the actual sun).

Once upon a time, an old story says, there was a king called Midas, who had at least one weakness, he was far too fond of money. One day a stranger who could perform magic, offered to give this king any gift he might desire. "Grant that everything I touch might be turned to gold," requested the greedy king without thinking very much about the matter. To his astonishment he noticed that the chair on which he was sitting had turned to gold but the man of magic had vanished. It was too late for the king to change his mind. The king dashed from object to object in the room, touching them all, turning them all into gold. Then he ran throughout the palace, transforming everything with his golden touch.

(SHOW GOLDEN OBJECTS AS YOU DESCRIBE THIS HAPPENING).

He even visited the rose garden and turned every petal to solid gold. "O, what a lucky fellow I am," he laughed. "I am easily the wealthiest and happiest man in the whole world. But all this running about has improved my appetite, I must have food and wine." Soon food and wine were brought to the king. Thirstily he raised the glass to his lips, but before he could swallow the wine it had turned to gold, even as his lips touched it.

Alas! Now the king realised that although he was certainly the richest man in the world, he was by no stretch of the imagination, the happiest, indeed, he knew he was in peril of starving to death. To make matters worse, his lovely young

daughter came into the room, and she was weeping.
"Whatever has happened to the roses, Daddy"? she
asked, "Someone has cast a horrible spell over
them, all their beautiful colours have vanished
and they have no more scent." Thinking to comfort
his child, the king drew her into his arms, and
she too turned to gold. Just at that moment the
magic man returned and he asked his majesty if he
still preferred gold to all else in the world. I
am sure you can guess his answer; a big loud "No".
Seeing that the king had learned his lesson, the
man of magic broke the spell so that everything
became as it once was.

There are a great many people in the world
like Midas, they are very good at making a lot of
money. When folk do this we often say they have
the golden touch. A great many people think that
if only they were rich they would be happy, but
the king's golden touch made him very <u>unhappy</u>.
He discovered that there are many things in life
which are <u>far</u> more important than money. He
discovered that people meant more to him than
things.

The truth is that it isn't the golden touch
which makes people happy, it is what I'm going to
call the Sunshine Touch. The people who have it
bring happiness and love into the lives of others.
More than anyone else in the world, Jesus had the
Sunshine Touch. Do you remember how Jesus fed
thousands of hungry people with five loaves and
two fishes? His fingers had the sunshine touch.
At a wedding party Jesus used His sunshine touch
again and turned water into the much needed wine.
Even when people were very sad, Jesus was able to
bring the sunshine of His love into their lives.
When Jesus hung on the cruel cross, one of the
thieves who was crucified beside Him felt that
Jesus would help him; he had been a wicked man
but now he was sorry for his sins. Jesus said

such wonderful words to him.."This day shalt thou
be with me in Paradise."

Boys and girls, you would not like to have
the same golden touch as Midas, would you? But
you _can_ have something far greater. You can have
the sunshine touch. Sometimes you sing....

"I'll be a sunbeam for Jesus,
And shine for Him each day,
In every way try to please Him,
At home, at school, at play".

This hymn is all about bringing the sunshine of
happiness to all you meet, it may take the form
of a kind word, a cheery smile, or a helpful action. I heard of a very young person who went into
the home of an old lady who was ill in bed. She
was cold, miserable and friendless until this boy
made her a roaring fire, and did many other
things he thought of to help her. He was a boy
with the sunshine touch.

Perhaps you would like to know how you can
obtain this wonderful gift, the sunshine touch.

First, only those with clean hearts can
really have it, you cannot spread sunshine and
sin at the same time,so you must ask God to help
you turn your back on doing wrong. You must ask
Jesus to come and live in your heart, that means
give Him your life, trying, with His Help, to
please Him in all you think and say and do. Why
should you do this? Because Jesus loves you. He
loves you enough to have died for you on the
cross to take the punishment for your sins. Ask
Jesus to come into your heart today. He will save
you from sin and give you the power to keep you
from doing wrong things. When you have done this
you will find you have received the gift of the
sunshine touch. (SHOW GOLDEN OBJECTS AND SKETCH OF THE SUN).

There is something far better than silver or
gold, there is something which will make you far
happier than the golden touch, it is the sunshine
touch. I pray that all of you will seek to obtain
this wonderful gift.

The Story Of Coral.

(SHOW CORAL).

Can anyone tell me what this is? Yes, Coral.
It has come from a place thousands of miles from
here, probably from the seas around Australia. It
is very hard and brittle to feel.

In the warm waters of tropical regions,live
millions of little creatures, so small you would
hardly notice them,   when young they swim about
in the sea. God has designed each of these little creatures to be a builder so one day these
little creatures fasten themselves to the rock
and never leave it again.   As the salt water
washes over them,   they put out little feelers,
and feed upon the tiny particles of food to be
found in the ocean. Each little creature builds
for itself a layer of protection, and when the
creature dies the flesh rots away until only
this shell of protection is left. You could say
that this protection is their skeleton which op-
posite to us is on the outside. It is these masses and masses of skeletons which we call coral.

(SHOW CORAL AGAIN).

Some coral is beautifully coloured and
looks like a garden of flowers under the sea. In
time,   the pieces of coral become very tightly
pressed together so that they become as hard as
stone, houses can be built of coral. More wonderful still,   as each piece of coral rests upon
more coral underneath, new islands appear, growing up out of the sea, which become big enough
to live on and build houses and grow vegetables.
So the coral which is so useful is really compo-
sed of millions of tiny builders, each so small
that if he worked alone,   his efforts would be
useless, yet because he works with others he can
build an island.

Boys and girls who are working for God,
often feel they cannot do very much, - not nearly so much as the grown-ups. But if they are all
working together, they can do a great deal. God
is watching all you do and He notices what you
have done for love of Him and He will send others to help you.   Before you know what is happ-

ening, you will find that you and they together
are building God's temple.   What do we mean by
the Temple of God?   God says that those who belong to Him are His building, His church,   His
temple,   this is because He lives in the hearts
of those who love Him and He is _in_ them, just as
you live in a house.   To help you understand
what I mean, I will tell you a true story.   A
young teacher was working in a school in the
South West of England, it was war time and many
children were sent to live in that village to
escape the bombs which were falling on London.
In her class was a boy named Nickoll who was
nine years old. He listened very attentively to
what his new teacher had to say about Jesus. He
understood that he had done many wrong things
and was very sorry about this, so he asked Jesus
to forgive him and be his Saviour and friend.
Jesus knew that Nickoll really meant what he
said and he became a Christian and wanted to
share his new life and hope of heaven. He made
up his mind to do his best to make sure his
friends and relations would meet him there.   So
Nickoll became one of God's builders, he told
his friends that they needed to give their lives
to God.

        One day his Uncle, who was in the Navy, came
to stay for a month at the farm where Nickoll
was.   Nickoll went around alot with his Uncle
and told him all that Jesus meant for him.   His
Uncle became very interested and went into the
nearest town to buy a New Testament so that he
could find out more about Jesus, and how to get
to Heaven.   Soon it was time for him to rejoin
his ship and Nickoll was very sad when his Uncle
went away.

        One day, some time later, Nickoll said to
his teacher, "Miss! Guess what? I've had a let-

ter from my Uncle and he says he has become a Christian!" The teacher and the rest of the class were thrilled to hear this news. Later on Nickoll had another letter from his Uncle to say that he had been speaking to some of the other sailors and three of them had given their hearts to Jesus and were meeting each day to talk to Jesus and read the Bible.

So you see Nickoll was a real builder for God, wasn't he? Just as a builder adds one brick upon another, so Nickoll was the means of adding souls to the Kingdom of God. He was only nine years of age but because he did his part and won his Uncle for Jesus, God was able to use that sailor to win three others. We shall never know the end of Nickoll's story. Who knows? Perhaps those three sailors won others?

(SHOW CORAL AGAIN).

So everytime you see a piece of coral, think of the millions of tiny builders who made it. Then ask Jesus to make you a builder....a boy or a girl who wins others to Him. Then you will be able to sing from your heart that lovely chorus: -

"We are building today,
In our work and in our play...."

THE SALMON.

AIM OF LESSON.....To show the necessity of resisting temptation and
not "going with the crowd."

OBJECT NEEDED.....A tin of salmon or a picture of a salmon.

Daddy always made the tea for Mummy and
Dorothy and Tom on Sundays. When they came home
from Sunday School, they went for a little walk
to give them a good appetite for their tea. Not
that <u>Tom</u> needed to work up an appetite, he always
had one! When they were out, Daddy always made
what he called "his surprise tea". Sometimes he
would have some tasty pork sausages on sticks.
In the summer time it might be strawberries and
cream. Sometimes he had a chocolate cake on the
table. One week they came home extra hungry and
heard Daddy hammering away in the kitchen.

Dorothy said,"It sounds as though Daddy is opening a tin of peaches.......or pears." Young Tom
just couldn't wait any longer so he looked round
the kitchen door and saw Daddy at work on a tin
just like this......

(SHOW TIN OF SALMON).

     "Oh! Salmon," cried Tom in delight. I love
salmon.   It's so tasty." "It looks so pretty,"
added Dorothy who liked her food to look attrac-
tive.   "It's a shame to eat it really," said
Daddy thoughtfully.   "The salmon is a wonderful
fish; in fact, I would like you two children to
be like this fish......before it is put into the
tin of course!"   The children giggled, Dorothy
said, "What do you mean Daddy?" Daddy replied,
"Of course, I didn't mean I want you to look
like a fish,but in some ways I would like you to
behave like a salmon." "Well, I can swim pretty
well.   Bet I could beat any boy in my class,"
boasted Tom.   "I didn't mean swim like a fish,
either," laughed Daddy.   "Any fish, if it is
alive at all, can swim.   It's the direction in
which it swims which is important.

     Let me tell you the true story of a salmon.
We could pretend it was the sister of this one
before it got into the tin.   Once upon a time,
the salmon lived out in the big ocean, but one
day she felt a tremendous wish to leave the sea
and swim up one of the rivers.   She didn't know
why she felt this great urge to do this,   she
just knew it was the one and only thing she wanted to do.   It was really God the great creator
who made the fish feel this way,   because it is
the clear shallow river water in which the salmon must lay her eggs. So one day, this salmon
and thousands and thousands more, left the great
salty ocean and began to swim up a long narrow
river. This sounds easy enough but the fish had

to swim against fast flowing currents. Sometimes
fishermen tempted her with bait, but on all that
long journey she ate nothing and got thinner and
thinner.   She was not going to risk getting
caught until she had found the quiet, peaceful
waters she was looking for. Sometimes, a waterfall blocked her path and then the fish would
take a great leap into the air...sometimes leap-
ing more than six feet to get to the other side
of the waterfall. Then, at last,thin and weary,
she reached a quiet beautiful stretch of water
she needed so much."

     "I think I see now what you meant about
wanting us to be like this salmon",said Dorothy.
"Any old rubbish or any dead fish can float down
the river, but it takes a real live fish who
never gives up, to swim up the steam."   "Yes,"
said Daddy,   "Now that you are both Christians,
having given your hearts to Jesus, sometimes it
will seem as though everyone is against you. It
is so easy to do something just because all your
chums are doing it, it's so hard to say, "No",
when someone offers you that first cigarette, or
that first drink or worse still, that first try
of drugs.   It's so hard to say "No", when the
rest of the gang are up to mischief. It's just
as hard for you as for that salmon swimming
against the stream.   Remember, it was God who
gave the salmon the urge to go up the river and
it was God who gave her the power to do so.   In
the same way,   it is God who will give you the
power to say "No", when everyone else is saying
"Yes".   When the salmon found her lovely quiet
resting place where she could lay her eggs, she
was satisfied.   When all the temptations and
difficulties of life are over, you will be pleased and satisfied,for you will be in Heaven with
Jesus.

There is a story in the Bible about some boys who were brave and determined like the salmon. Once, the Jews were beaten in battle by the Babylonians and many of them were taken away as prisoners. The heathen king treated them well,even offering them wine from his own table, which most of them were only too pleased to accept. But Daniel, one of the captives, and his friends remained true to God. They said, "No", and risked the king's anger. In God's book, He has promised this. "Them that honour me, I will honour." Daniel and his friends became great friends and favourites of the king and in the end, Daniel became almost as important as the king himself. Most important of all, God was pleased with him. If Daniel had been like the rest of the Jews who were afraid to say "No",no-one would ever have heard of him."

(HOLD UP TIN OF SALMON).

Boys and girls if the salmon on the label could talk, perhaps he would say, "Be like my brothers and sisters who had the courage to press on up the stream against all difficulties. I was the one who gave in. See what became of me." When you have salmon for tea, ask God to make you brave and determined.

Any dead fish can float with the stream, but it takes a live fish to swim against it.

THE TWO GIFTS

AIM OF LESSON.....To show that only in Christ is found lasting
pleasure.

OBJECTS NEEDED.....Bubble mixture and pipe or Bubble ring usually
supplied with Bubble Tin.

A rubber ball.

Jean and Tom were two very young children and their favourite Uncle was called Uncle Sam. One day he came to stay with them and he bought them both a present, he gave Jean something like this....

(UNWRAP TIN OF BUBBLE MIXTURE AND SHOW CHILDREN).

Jean was delighted when Uncle told her how to make beautiful bubbles and watch them float away. Tom hoped that he would be given some bubble mixture too, but to his surprise, Uncle gave him a different present. (HOLD UP RUBBER BALL).

Then I'm afraid Tom said something very rude, he
said,   "I don't want an old ball,   I want some
bubble mixture,like Jean's." He stamped his foot
and ran away leaving his ball on the carpet.Jean
had a lovely time blowing bubbles. Look! This is
how she did it.

(BLOW SOME BUBBLES FOR THE CHILDREN TO SEE).

Jean   tried   to   catch some of them but when her
fingers touched them, they disappeared......like
this.

(BLOW A FEW MORE BUBBLES AND LET THE CHILDREN TOUCH THEM).

     "They   don't   last very long,   Uncle," she
said sadly.   Then she cheered up.   "Never mind,
I can easily make some more."   So she blew and
blew and blew,   until all the bubble mixture was
gone and she had nothing left but an empty tin.

     Presently Tom came in.   "Where are all your
bubbles?" he asked.   "O they have all gone. I
tried to keep some of them,   but it was no use.
They just disappeared."   Then that naughty boy
began to laugh. "Ha! Ha! Your fine present has
all gone, you have nothing left, but my present
will last for years and years and years.   I can
play with it when ever I like.   I think I got
the best present after all."

     Poor Jean was so upset she began to cry.
After all she was very young and she couldn't
understand why bubbles can't last,.......at least
not until Uncle told her the reason. He explained it like this....."You see, Jean those bubbles
you made had a very fine soap skin, but inside
they were quite hollow,   they were filled with
nothing but air. They were never meant to last,
they just looked pretty for a few moments,that's
all.   Tom's ball is made of good hard,   solid

rubber.   It will never burst or disappear,   it
will give him pleasure for as long as he wants
to play with it."

       Then Uncle put his arms round the two of
them, you see, Uncle was a Christian and he knew
a lot of things. He said, "There are a lot of
things in this world which are like bubbles, they
are pretty and exciting and we think they are
going to make us very happy,   but we find these
things don't please us for long. There is really
nothing in them to make us happy, grown-ups say
these things are "Hollow.".........just like your
bubbles.

       There is One Person and only One who can
give us joy that will last, something which your
ball did, Tom. If you ask Jesus into your heart
He will give you joy which will last for ever.
When we ask Jesus to forgive us our sins, and
tell Him how much we love Him because He died
for us,   we become truly happy.   We are happy
because one day we are going to Heaven.   We are
happy because Jesus is our friend and is always
looking after us.   It is Satan, our enemy, who
likes to give us things or make us do things
which in the end only disappoint us, his pleas-
ures are not lasting........like Jean's bubbles.
Jesus gives us the really good things in life,
best of all, he gives us Himself."

AIMS OF LESSON.....To show the harmful nature of bad habits.
                   With Christ's help, to promote good habits.

OBJECTS NEEDED......Any kind of steel chain.
                    Gold or brass chain.

                    1st Poster: - "YOU" written in a circle on the
                                   left hand side, bound with a chain
                                   to "SIN" written on the right
                                   hand side.
                    Written over drawing of chain the word "HABIT".

                    2nd Poster: - The word "YOU" as before on left
                                   hand side in circle.
                                   The word "GOD" written in right
                                   hand circle.
                    A gold coloured chain with word "HABIT" written
                    over it, joining the two circles.

        Tommy was nine years of age. He was on his
way home from school with his friend Trevor, who
was two years older than he was.   "Guess what
I've got in my pocket?" asked Trevor.
"Water pistol?" guessed Tommy.
"No."
"A catapult?"
"No, I'll tell you. A couple of cigarettes."
"Where did you get them from?" asked Tommy, well

knowing that Trevor was forbidden to smoke. "Oh in that little shop across the road. The man in there often opens up a packet and sells them loose...Here try one."
"No thanks," said Tommy. "My dad says that smoking gives you cancer."
"Don't listen to him. All the rest of the boys do it. My big brother smokes and it doesn't seem to do him any harm."
"All right, but suppose my Dad finds out?"
"That's O.K. You will have finished it before you get home."

So Tommy smoked his first cigarette. It was not long before he was smoking several a day and he began to get a real craving for them.

At first no one noticed. Mummy was very busy and Daddy was often working late. Then Daddy caught a bad cold and he stayed home to get rid of it. When Tommy came home from school he was very surprised to see Daddy sitting in front of the fire and drinking some hot tea. Tommy held out his hands in front of the fire to warm them. "Hey," cried Daddy. "What are those brown stains on your fingers? Don't try to hide them. Here, let me see. Those are nicotine stains, left by the poison in cigarettes," he said gravely. "Poison?" cried Tommy. "I didn't know there was poison in cigarettes." "There are about nineteen different kinds of poisons in a cigarette and that is why I've told you over and over again not to start smoking. Not so long ago a little boy about your age, had been smoking, and he became so ill he had to be taken to hospital. He was in great pain because he could hardly breathe..How long have you been smoking?"
"I can't remember. It must be some time now."
"Then you will find them hard to give up. You know, smoking can cause a terrible disease call-

ed cancer, which can give you a slow and painful
death. Not only that, but smoking is a waste of
money....money which I cannot afford to give you.
Smoking is a very bad habit. Do you know what a
habit is?"   "Yes," said Tommy, "It's something
you have got to keep on doing." "That's right,"
agreed Daddy.   "A bad habit is like a strong
steel chain, which ties you to some sin, so that
you cannot tear yourself away from it."

(SHOW CHILDREN STEEL CHAIN).

    "There are many things which we do so often
that we do not realise they are becoming habits
which we cannot break. Carelessness in the way
you dress or do your work can become a habit.
Telling lies can become a habit.   Almost any
action,   if repeated often enough can become a
habit.

(SHOW CHILDREN FIRST POSTER).

But there is another wonderful chain you can
make.   It's the chain of good habits.   We can
think of it as a gold chain.   It can link us to
God.

(SHOW GOLD CHAIN).

Every time you make good habits, like praying
and reading your Bible, they become like a chain
which links you to God."

(SHOW CHILDREN SECOND POSTER).

    "Oh Daddy," said Tommy.   "I wish I could
get rid of my bad habits.   I would like my life
to be like that second chain, tied on to God."
"Well," said Daddy,   "There is a story in the
Bible, which is so up to date, it might have
been written just for you.   It tells you of the
One Person who can smash that chain of yours and
set you free. Listen!"

"There was once a follower of the Lord Jesus Christ who was called Peter. He was put in prison because he would not give up the Lord Jesus. In those days prisons were horrible places......stone floors, damp walls, rats running around, and very dark. To make matters worse, Peter was chained to two soldiers by the wrists, one on either side of him. How uncomfortable he must have felt. Peter had some very good friends and they heard of his plight. They helped him by praying for him. God answered their prayers with a miracle; in the middle of the night an angel visited Peter in prison, struck off his chains and led him to safety." Turning to Tommy, Daddy said, "Why not ask the Lord Jesus Christ to take charge of your life?" Tell Him you are sorry for the wrong things you have done, tell Him you are sorry you are chained by smoking. If you do this, Jesus will take away your wish to smoke. More than that, He will help you to form the golden chain of good habits, which will help to keep you close to Him. Will you let Him do this?"

Tommy saw that his Daddy really did know best. He found that when he gave his life to Jesus, he lost the old habits and made good ones in their place.

Boys and girls, don't be like the old Tommy.

(SHOW POSTER 1).

Make a change. Be like the new Tommy.

(SHOW POSTER 2).

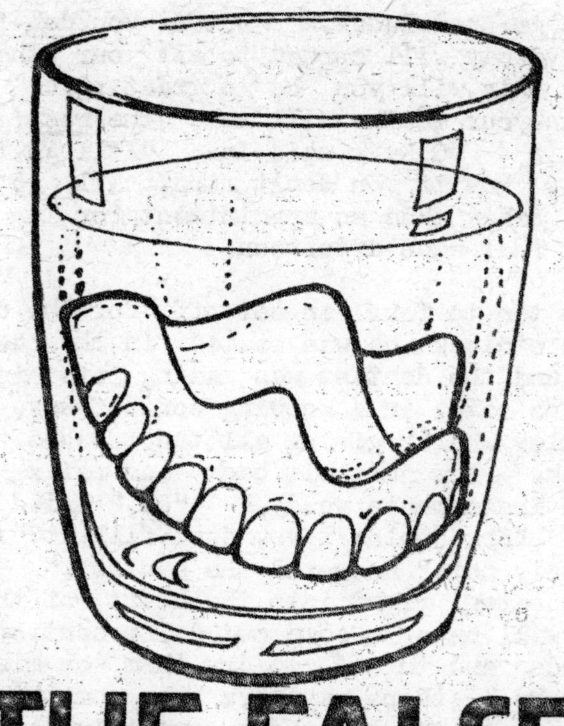

THE FALSE TEETH

AIM OF LESSON......To show that Jesus is the only One who can help us get rid of our sin.

OBJECT NEEDED.......Set of false teeth or drawing of false teeth.

Ian had a bad tooth.....a large one right at the back of his mouth and his Daddy said it must come out. "Why must I have it pulled out," questioned Ian.   "It only hurts now and then and I hate going to the dentist."   "I know all about

that," grinned Daddy. "But if you <u>don't</u> get it
out the decay will spread to all your other teeth
and not only will you be in great pain, but the
decay in your mouth will make the <u>rest</u> of your
body ill." O.K." said Ian, "I'll go to the
dentist, but if you don't mind, I'll go by myself." Daddy made an appointment for Ian at four
o'clock that same afternoon.

At ten to four Ian set off for the dentist,
by four o'clock he was seated in the dentist's
chair and the dentist was gazing into his mouth.
"Ahh," he said, in a knowing sort of way, "I see
the fellow who is giving all the trouble, away at
the back. Now just sit back and relax while I
get the instruments ready." "Oh," cried Ian alarmed. "Er..couldn't you just fill it?" "No,
definitely not," answered the dentist." "The decay has eaten right into the heart of the tooth
and it will have to come out." The dentist washed
his hands and turned to dry them on his roller
towel. Well, there may have been something wrong
with Ian's tooth, but there certainly wasn't anything wrong with his legs! When the dentist turned round again, Ian had gone.

Soon afterwards he came home. "You're home
early," exclaimed his mother. "Open your mouth
and let me see," "No," cried Ian. "It hurts too
much, oh! it's sore." "Ah well," replied mother,
"It will soon feel better, I expect you are glad
to get rid of it." "Yes I am," said Ian. Of
course Ian had told a lie and I'm sorry to have
to tell you that he often told them, it had become a habit.

Later Daddy came home. Daddy knew Ian a lot
better than Mum. It wasn't long before he was
having a good look at Ian's mouth. "Why! you
naughty boy," he cried, "You didn't get it out at

all. What is more, you told a lie about it. Not
only will that tooth <u>have</u> to come out but you
will have to get rid of that habit of telling
lies. Lying is a sin and sin spreads, just as
much as tooth decay.   I'll make another appointment for you on Saturday and this time I'll take
you myself."

    Ian could see that his father was really up-
set not so much because he had run away from the
dentist, but because he had once more told a lie.
He had often tried to stop telling lies, but he
couldn't, it had become a habit.   He found it
just as easy to tell lies as to tell the truth.
That afternoon he was chosen to represent his
class in the Junior school soccer team. The master bundled all the boys on to the school bus and
drove them away to another school.   There the
boys went into the changing room to put on their
football togs. Suddenly Ian had the shock of his
life.   One of the other team put his hand to his
mouth and took out a set of false teeth. Then he
asked the master if he would mind looking after
them. (SHOW FALSE TEETH).

Ian just gaped at the boy and then he stammered,
"How do you come to have false teeth, and at your
age? Why did you take them out?"   "Stupid," he
retorted, "Because I had a bad tooth and would —
n't have it out.   The decay just spread to the
others and then I had to have them all out and
have false ones.   It's dangerous to play wearing
false teeth, so that is why I take them out."

    Ian found it hard to concentrate on the ball
after that. How awful if he should have to have
<u>all</u> his teeth out instead of only one.   As for
wearing false teeth, that would be terrible,after
all he was only eleven. Still, the other boy was
only eleven and it had happened to him!

At teatime Ian was very quiet. "A penny for your thoughts," smiled mother. "Well, as a matter of fact I met a boy today who wears false teeth."

(SHOW FALSE TEETH AGAIN).

Turning to his father he said, "I'll not wait till Saturday to see the dentist, I'd like to go as soon as possible." Daddy was very pleased to hear his decision. "And," continued Ian, "I'm sorry I've got into the habit of telling lies. I want to get rid of that habit, but I don't know how." How do you get rid of a bad tooth?" asked Daddy. "Why go to a chap who can take it out, of course." "Yes," answered his father. "In the same way you will have to go to a person who can rid you of lying and all your other sins, that person is Jesus Christ. He can do for you what you can't do for yourself. You couldn't pull out your own teeth, could you?" "Course not," laughed Ian. "Just ask Jesus to forgive your sin. When He forgives you, He removes your sin as far as the east is from the west. That's another way of saying your sins are removed for ever. Ask Him to come by His Spirit, and live in your heart. He will come if you really _want_ to have no more to do with sin. He will take away your habit of lying and will give you a real desire and power to tell the truth."

Ian found his father had been speaking the truth and I'm sure if Ian were here today, he would say, "Come to Jesus, Give Him your life..He will give you a clean heart and the power to please God and grow like Jesus." So, boys and girls, every time you clean your teeth or see a set of false teeth, remember the story you heard today.

THE FISH.

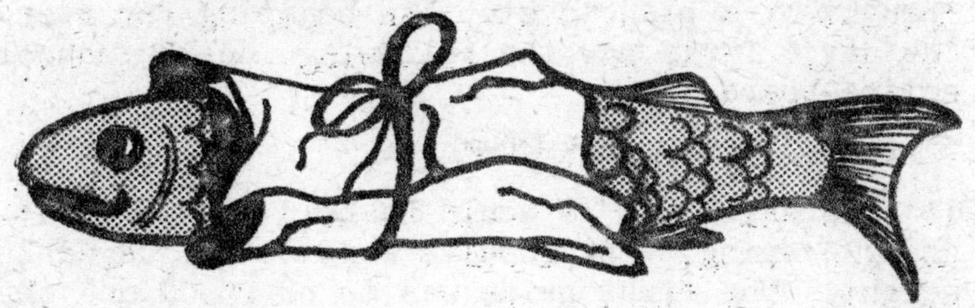

AIM OF LESSON.....To show that man looks on the outward appearance but God looks for a pure heart.

OBJECTS NEEDED.....A fish or toy fish, wrapped in a parcel.

The words "FISHING COMPETITION".

David liked to go fishing on his holidays and when it was time to go back home he felt very sad. However, he was looking forward to September, with keen anticipation to starting life in a new school. When at the school, to his great surprise and delight one of the boys asked him if he would like to join the school fishing club. Of course he joined and every Saturday he went with a few other boys to fish. He had not been in the club long before he discovered that one of the other members, called John, was always boasting of the big fish he could catch. The strange thing about the whole matter was that no one else had actually <u>seen</u> him catch one of these monsters. He often came into the class room stretching out his arms like this, saying, "Say, you should have seen the big fish I caught last night. It was as big as this." Every time

he told this story, the fishes he caught seemed
to get bigger and bigger and bigger.

        The other boys grew tired of his boasting
and Bruce, the leader of the fishing club
thought of a plan to stop his boasting for ever.
One day, David saw the following on the school
notice-board.....

(SHOW WORDS..."FISHING COMPETITION").

It also said that it would be held the next Saturday evening. The results were to be judged by
weight. The first prize was to be £5.00 and the
second prize £3.00.

        David, John and the rest of the class went
out next Saturday to fish.   John was not only a
boastful boy, he was also very greedy, and when
he saw how small were the fish he was catching,
he walked slowly away from the other boys and
when he was out of sight he ran home. He crept
in through the pantry window because he knew
that inside the pantry was a huge fish his father had caught the night before. He picked it up
and wrapped it in a piece of brown paper.   It
looked like this.....

(SHOW PARCEL CONTAINING FISH).

He went back to the boys who were now all laying
out their fishes for inspection.   When no one
was looking, John slipped in his own fish among
the rest of his catch. Presently the judge came
along.   When he came to John he glanced at his
fishes.   John's heart thumped! He felt certain
of victory.   Why he could see that his fish was
by far the largest.   It looked something like
this, only bigger.

(UNWRAP PARCEL AND SHOW FISH).

The judge just shook his head and passed on down the row of boys and their fishes, presently it was David's turn to be amazed. He picked up the very smallest fish David had caught. "David is the winner," he announced and in due time, he received first prize. John could not hide his astonishment, jealousy and anger. "It's not fair," he blurted out. "Why, any one can see my fish is the biggest. It said on the notice-board, "Results to be judged by weight and mine is the biggest."

The judge shook his head. "That's right... by weight, but this competition is kind of different...the prize goes to the smallest.......the lightest fish. Not the biggest. It didn't say what kind of weight, did it?" No, it was not the biggest. <u>That's not what I was looking for.</u>"

Then, of course, John realised that the whole matter had been a trick to show him up and for the rest of his life he would never again boast of the big fish he could catch. It was a very thoughtful boy who put the fish back on its plate again in the pantry.

(HOLD UP FISH).

The story of the fish has something to teach us, in fact it reminds me of a man of God who once set out to choose a king. He found a man with seven sons, six of them came for his inspection, beginning with the eldest. The eldest was so tall and good looking that the prophet thought he must be the man of God's choice, but God gave his judgement on the matter. He told Samuel, the man of God, that He wasn't looking for anything this son had. In fact God said the same about all six of them. Samuel must have wondered just what God WAS looking for. Then the youngest passed before him. He was very young and not as powerful looking as his brothers yet God told Samuel that this young lad was the king he had chosen. "Man looketh on the outward appearance," God said,"But God looks on the heart."

Boys and girls, one day you will come face to face with Jesus. Will He be pleased with what He sees? Perhaps you are thinking, "Well, I'm sure to please God, my Mum and Dad make me go to Sunday School and to church, as well." But that isn't what God is looking for. Others of you may think, "I'm sure to be O.K. I say my prayers every night and sometimes I read my Bible." But _that_ isn't what God is looking for. Or someone may be saying much the same as the boy in the nursery rhyme. "What a good boy am I". But that is not what God is looking for.

What _is_ God looking for? He is looking for a pure heart. That means God wants boys and girls to turn away from what is wrong and ask God to forgive them. He wants boys and girls to ask Him to live in their hearts, then He will help us to live lives pleasing to Him. Only those with Jesus in their hearts will one day go to Heaven.

Have you asked Jesus in yet? He died to take the punishment for your sins. Now He is alive and although you cannot see Him is with you.

So, everytime you see a fish or eat a fish or catch a fish, let it remind you of this....It isn't size or looks or brains or strength God is looking for, it is a pure heart. Your heart will only become pure in His sight when it is the home of the Lord Jesus Christ. Make sure He lives in you, invite Him in now.....

The Magic Sword.

```
AIM OF LESSON.......To show there is one, and only one, Saviour.
```

```
OBJECTS NEEDED.......A toy sword.
                     A Bible.
```

Hundreds of years ago in Ancient Britain, a prince called Arthur, was born. Although everyone was very glad to hear of his birth, one wise old magician realised that the baby prince would have many enemies who would seek his life. Therefore, he begged to be allowed to take the child away to be put in the charge of a good old knight called Sir Hector.   So Arthur was brought up as his own son, with his own two sons, Sir Kay and Sir Tor.

One day the old king died and many nobles claimed the throne of Britain.   No one could be found wise enough to settle the dispute as to who was the true king and it was very important that the right man should be chosen.   The new king ought to be good and kind but at the same time he should be very strong, so that he could lead his men in battle against Britain's enemies.

The Archbishop of Canterbury, whose duty it was to crown the new king, was at his wits end, when one day he had a visit from an old magician, Merlin, who told him to get all those who claimed the throne into the great cathedral. While they were there, a steel anvil mysteriously appeared in the churchyard. This anvil was thrust through with a fine sword. It was something like this one here.

(SHOW SWORD).

It was no ordinary sword. It was very sharp and its hilt was studded with jewels. There was writing on its hilt. Wait a moment and I'll read you the strange message.

(HOLD SWORD TO EYE LEVEL AND PRETEND TO READ).

"Whoever can pull this sword from the anvil is the rightful king of Britain."

Now Sir Hector, his sons, Sir Kay and Sir Tor and Prince Arthur had also come to London. One day as they rode out, Sir Kay found he had left his sword behind in his lodgings. He asked young Arthur to fetch it, but no one was at home. So Arthur rode back to rejoin Sir Kay. As he rode past the churchyard he noticed the sword still in the anvil, for no one had yet been strong enough to pull it out. As he had not been in London long enough to hear about the sword, he leapt from his horse and seized the splendid sword. With scarcely any effort he pulled it out and gave it to Sir Kay.

(PRETEND TO PULL OUT SWORD AND BRANDISH IT AS YOU TALK).

Sir Kay very well knew the meaning of the story of the sword and he told his old father that he had drawn it out. Sir Hector was not so easily deceived so he forced his son to confess that it was Arthur who had drawn the sword. The sword was replaced in the anvil where it seemed stuck fast once more.   Many tried to draw it but were not able.

(ACT THIS).

Only Arthur was able to do it.

(PRETEND TO DO THIS AND HOLD IT HIGH).

Arthur had proved himself to be the true king and with the help of his wonderful sword, he was able to save Britain from her enemies. He was the _only_ one brave enough, good enough and wise enough to save his country.   No other man could do this, only Arthur could pass the test.

Boys and girls, I want to tell you today, of another King who wants to be your _Saviour_, His name is King Jesus. The Bible says that there is only one name given under Heaven by which we must be saved.   This means that only Jesus and Jesus _only_ can save us from our great enemy, the devil, or Satan as he is also called, and take us eventually to heaven.   King Jesus died in your place to take the punishment you deserve for your sins. He did this because He loved you so much, He is the only One who can save you and give you a new life.   Just tell Him how glad you are He died for you and invite Him into your life and then with His help you will live the rest of your life to please Him.

You may be thinking, "It is so hard to live for Jesus, when Satan tempts me to do bad things or say bad words. Somehow I just do them. It was all very well for Arthur, he had a wonderful sword to help him."

Boys and girls, did you know that God HAS given you a sword? Here it is.

(HOLD UP BIBLE).

The other name for God's book is "The sword of
the Spirit." Now a sword like this one would be
of no use at all against Satan,

(HOLD UP TOY SWORD).

because he is invisble. Therefore God has given
you an invisible sword which are words from the
Bible. Sometimes Satan whispers in your mind,
"Get your own back, that boy played a nasty trick
on you. You get even with Him." When Satan says
this sort of thing just search God's Book for a
good answer. You could say to yourself and Satan,
"The Bible says, 'Love your enemies', I can't do
what you want Satan, Go away." That is the way to
use the sword of the Spirit; it is, in fact, much
more powerful than Arthur's magic sword.

Arthur had to practice his sword drill, and
know how to use it properly.

(MAKE A FEW THRUSTS WITH THE SWORD).

You will have to do the same with the sword of
the Spirit. Read the Bible. Ask your parents to
buy some Junior Bible Reading Notes, which will
help you to understand it and make it interesting
for you. If you cannot read well yet, ask Mummy
or Daddy to read to you from it each day.

This is a very fine sword.......

(HOLD UP SWORD).

But this one is far better.

(HOLD UP BIBLE).

Remember, before you can use it you must
join the King's army. Ask Jesus into your heart,
He will then be your king. Use the sword of the
Spirit and my prayer is that you may win many
battles for Jesus.

The Paper Ships

AIM OF LESSON........To show the danger of putting off salvation.

OBJECTS NEEDED........Some paper boats on a metal tray, one much larger than the others.

Jimmy was staying at the sea-side for his summer holidays where he attended a Beach Mission for children. They had a wonderful time in the mornings, building sand castles for competitions, treasure hunting, donkey riding, boating and many other exciting things. After lunch a man whom

the children called Uncle Bob, and his helpers,
gathered the children round him and showed them
beautiful pictures and told them exciting stories.
Many of these stores were about Jesus.

Jimmy learned that he and all other people
were sinners and that Jesus had died on a cruel
cross to take his punishment for the sins he had
committed. Uncle Bob asked the children to give
their lives to Jesus while they were still young.
Jimmy thought about all these things.   "I would
love to become a Christian and grow up to be a
fine man like Uncle Bob......I ought not to keep
putting it off....Suppose I got knocked down or
had a serious illness, I would die with my heart
still black with sin.   I would go to live with
Statn and not with Jesus in Heaven, that would
be dreadful." However, four weeks later Jimmy
still had not given his life to Jesus.

One morning Uncle Bob showed the children
how to make toy boats from old newspapers.

(SHOW ONE TO CHILDREN).

They were so easy to make and best of all
they didn't cost anything. Soon Jimmy had made a
whole fleet of boats and had great fun sailing
them round the moat of his sand castle.

When tea-time came, Jimmy went home but
before going to bed he made a big paper boat.

(SHOW BOAT).

Then he made a number of smaller boats.

(SHOW SMALLER BOATS).

"This big one is the liner and these small ones
are the tugs," he explained to his Daddy.

Jimmy had a strange dream that night when he
dreamed that his paper boats were sailing on the
open sea.   Suddenly they changed into the very
boats they were meant to represent.   There was
the liner. There were the tugs.

It all seemed so real that Jimmy could even
see the captain on the bridge, peering out to sea.
Everything was so calm and still. Suddenly Jimmy
noticed something which alarmed him. A tongue of
flame was coming through one of the lower port-
holes, worse still the captain seemed unaware of
what was happening.   Then a sailor rushed up on
deck and shouted up at the captain, "Fire! Fire!"
The captain looked down at the sailor and cried,
"What's all the fuss, get the fire fighting crew
to deal with it and leave me in peace."

The sailor disappeared below.   Soon he came
on deck again and shouted up at the captain. "We
have done all we can but the fire is out of cont-
rol, if we stay here any longer we'll be burned
to death."
(SET FIRE TO THE LARGE PAPER SHIP AS YOU TALK).

Then Jimmy heard the captain give the order to
abandon ship and one by one the little life boats
were lowered into the water, filled with members
of the crew and the passengers.   In his dream he
saw that the big ship was slowly sinking.   The
fire had taken rapid hold upon the ship and the
flames were fast spreading. Everyone had left the
ship but the Captain.   To Jimmy's surprise, he
didn't seem in any hurry at all! He came down
from the bridge and entered the cabin.   "I must
enter up my log book," Jimmy heard him mutter.
"There's still plenty of time".   He sat down and
calmly began to write.

All this time the fire below was raging
furiously. It would not be long before it reached
the lower deck, then the upper deck and finally

the cabin in which the captain was still sitting.
Just then, one of the little boats came back to
the big boat, it was the Captain's mate who had
come to plead with his Captain to leave the boat
before it was too late. "Quick! Jump, before it
is too late," he roared. "I'm coming", yelled
back the Captain. But he didn't leave his cabin.
He had suddenly remembered the men's wages in the
safe. "It would never do to leave all that money
behind", he thought. Meanwhile, the mate, scared
of being sucked under by the sinking ship, had
rowed away. He couldn't understand his captain
at all. By this time in his dream, Jimmy saw that
the flames had almost reached the cabin. "I must
do something to help him, before it is too late",
thought Jimmy in desperation. The dream was so
real that Jimmy sat up in bed and yelled, "Jump,
before it is too late!"

Then to Jimmy's horror, the Captain turned
and seemed to look straight at him. Somehow his
face changed, it became the face of Uncle Bob of
the seaside mission. "There is plenty of time,"
he laughed. "That's what you keep saying, isn't
it? Plenty of time." "Jump NOW, NOW, NOW,"
yelled Jimmy with all his might.

Suddenly Jimmy felt his mother's arms around
him and heard her say, "Whatever is the matter
Jimmy? You have had a nightmare and wakened us
all up." Jimmy told his mother the whole terrible
dream. "Mother," he cried, "I've been as stupid
as that captain. I have kept putting off becoming
a Christian."

Jimmy asked Jesus to forgive his sins and
come to live in his heart, to be his Saviour and
guide. How thrilled Uncle Bob was next day when
Jimmy told him. I do hope the boys and girls here
today will not be so foolish as the Captain in
Jimmy's dream. Won't you, like Jimmy, ask Jesus
to forgive you the sin that is in your heart and
be your Saviour and Friend. Why not do it today.

GOD'S TELEPHONE.

AIM OF LESSON.....To show the nature of prayer.

____

OBJECTS NEEDED.....A Toy TELEPHONE.
                   A BIBLE.

____

Raymond was very excited because a telephone had just been installed in his home.

(SHOW TELEPHONE).

"Can I use it whenever I like?" he asked. "Well", replied Daddy, "You can use it for anything important, but the 'phone costs an awful lot of money, every quarter I shall have to pay the Post Office for the use of it. It isn't free, it has to be paid for. However, I know of a free telephone that you can use whenever you like and the owner won't charge you as much as a penny." Of course Raymond wanted to know much more about this free telephone. So his father explained.

(PICK UP THE TELEPHONE AND POINT OUT THE PARTS AS YOU SPEAK).

"This phone is visible and it has wires connecting it with the exchange and other users. God has His own private telephone and it is invisible. It has no wires. The name of God's telephone is prayer."

"Once upon a time you were a sinner. But you were sorry for all the wrong things you had done. Jesus forgave you and you became His child. When you were a sinner you had no right to use God's phone, because sin cuts us off from God, but now that you are forgiven and your sins are washed away, you are no longer cut off from Him. Just as you can lift the receiver and talk to your friends, so you can talk to God in prayer.

Raymond thought quite a lot about God's telephone after that and he used it many times. Sometimes he used it to say "thank you" to God when he had had an exciting day, or when someone had given him a beautiful present. Sometimes he used it to tell Jesus he was sorry when he had done something wrong. He used it when he wanted God to do something special for somebody else. He found out that God's telephone had dozens of uses. He used his Daddy's phone a lot too, sometimes he would ring up a friend to see if he got the same answer as himself in his homework, or he would ring his friend Billy to see if he would come out and play with him or go for a walk.

One day Raymond came home from school with a very long face. "What's the matter, dear?" asked mother. "Oh," cried Raymond, "Billy said he rang up two days ago, to ask me to his party and he couldn't get through to me, so I missed the party. I think it's a rotten old phone, it lets you down, just when you most need it. It must have been out of order."

"No," smiled mother, "I'm afraid that's not the reason. Look what it says here in the directory. Always replace the receiver."

(SHOW RECEIVER).

"You see, Raymond the last time you called some-one else, you left the receiver lying on the table when you had finished.   That meant you were not connected with your friends.   You were out of touch and so you could not hear Billy's voice.   When Daddy came home Raymond told him the same sad story of how he had missed the party just because he had been out of touch. Daddy was very understanding about it all.

(PICK UP THE TELEPHONE).

"Yes," said Daddy, "It was a great pity you were out of touch, because you lost a lot of happin-ess. Do you remember me telling you about God's telephone?" "Yes, Daddy, I remember you said it was free and it was called "Prayer"."   "That's right", replied his father.   "And now I want to tell you more about God's phone.   YOU don't do all the talking! Often God wants to talk to you ....at the very least once a day." "But how can God talk to me?"   cried Billy quite astounded. "God uses His Book, the Holy Bible, to speak to you," explained Daddy.

(SHOW BIBLE AND OPEN IT).

"Here he tells you how he wants you to live. He gives you good advise and comforting words when you are sad.   Without reading and understanding this book you cannot be happy or successful."
"But Daddy, there is so much in the Bible I don't understand," broke in Billy.   "I know, I know," replied his father.   "But God will help you to understand more and more as time passes. I will also help you by buying you the Junior Scripture Union Notes."

Daddy did as he had promised. From then on
Raymond read his Bible every day...well...almost
every day.   Like all boys he sometimes forgot.
The notes helped to explain the hard parts and
made the Bible a very interesting book.

I wonder boys and girls, have you a telephone in your home?   Not the kind that rings a
bell.

(RING BELL).

Have you started to use the free telephone I
call prayer?   Remember,   it isn't just a one-
sided conversation. Have you given God a chance
to get on the other side of the line by reading
your Bible every day?

Remember how Raymond missed a party by
failing to keep in touch?

You, too, will miss all that is good and
best in life,   if you do not keep in touch on
God's telephone.

A FEATHER PILLOW.

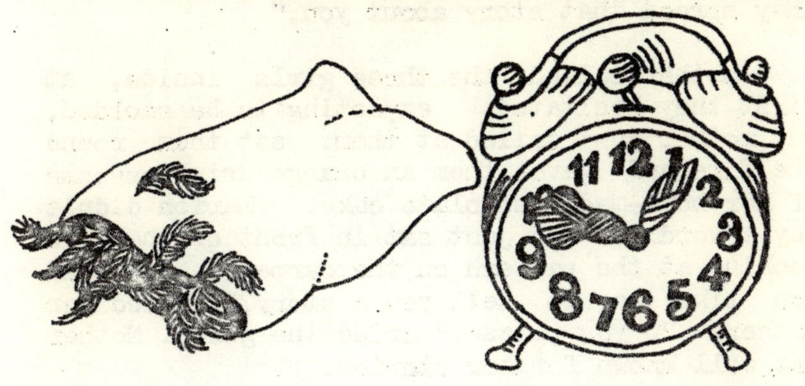

AIM OF LESSON.....To show the powers of the tongue for either
                  good or evil.

OBJECTS NEEDED.....A pillow filled with feathers with an opening
                   at one end.
                   A Bible.
                   A clock or watch.

Marion came running home from school one day in tears. "Whatever is the matter?" asked her mother. "All the girls say I cheated in the arithmetic exam and I didn't, I didn't," she sobbed. "But _why_ are all the girls saying such horrid things," her mother wanted to know. "Well," cried Marion, "I happened to put the same answers as Betty Brown and she told Anne Simpson I was sitting next to her and that I _might_ have copied, then Anne told Mary Cooper that I _had_ copied the answers and now all the girls think I am a cheat." Just then Mother happened to glance out of the window. "I can see Anne and Betty and Mary out there skipping, I'll call them in." "O don't do that, or they will say I have been telling tales," Marion begged. "You need not worry", answered her Mother, "They are just ordinary girls like yourself, but they were thoughtless and careless and didn't stop to think before they spread that story about you."

Mother called the three girls inside, at first they hesitated, expecting to be scolded, but mother just smiled at them, sat them round the fire and gave them an orange drink and some of her home-made chocolate cake. Marion didn't say a word. She just sat in front of the fire looking at the pattern on the carpet. "Would you like me to tell you a story?" asked her mother. "O yes please," cried the girls. Mother was well known for her stories.

"Once upon a time, there was a very good, kind, wise minister of a church. Everyone seemed to love him and his congregation grew bigger and bigger and bigger, but in his church there was a fellow who didn't know how to tame his tongue. (O yes......tongues have to be tamed and kept in check, just like a wild animal). This man, with the untamed tongue, said something very unkind about the minister and the man who listened to the nasty remarks repeated them to someone else, who repeated it to another, adding a bit more to the story. In time, the whole church heard the story and the whole district, until everyone thought the kind minister wasn't fit to be a minister at all. His reputation was ruined, the congregation got less and less, people didn't want to come to hear him any more, he was so broken hearted he became very ill.

The man who had started all these lies heard about his illness and he felt very sorry indeed for what he had done. He made up his mind to go and tell the good old minister how sorry he was for his tale bearing. The poor sick broken hearted man listened to his story in silence. At last he said, sadly, "O yes I'll forgive you.   But alas! You will never be able to undo all the harm you have done."

"O but I will, I will," broke in the man with the untamed tongue.   "I'll find everyone who knows the story and tell them it isn't true."

The ministers answer was to sit up in bed and reach for his pillow.   He ripped a hole in one end of it. (SHOW PILLOW).

"Open the window," he asked.   When the window was open, he took the feathers and threw handful after handful out of the window.   A strong wind blew them in all directions, on and on the feathers blew, over the gardens, into the woods beyond, the lighter ones being carried right out of sight. (THROW OUT A FEW FEATHERS).

"Now", said the minister, "You take this pillow-case and look for everyone of those feathers and put them all back again." "But that would be an impossible task, even now some of them are quite out of sight." "You are right," replied the minister.   "And it would be impossible for you to trace all the rumours and lies told about me and to replace them with the truth. Your tongue has done so much damage, you can never undo it. The best that you can do is to remember never, never to say an unkind or untrue word about anyone again for the rest of your life." There was an awkward silence after this story and then Betty began to weep and weep as though she would never stop. At last she said, "I know why you told us that story. It was because I said nasty things about Marion and now everyone believes them." The other two said that they had helped to spread the story.   "Is there nothing we can do, nothing at all?" sobbed Betty. "Yes, there is," comforted Marion's mother." "I can introduce you to Someone who can tame that wild ton-

gue of yours. His name is Jesus," Mother con -
tinued, "It isn't really the fault of your tongue.   When the clock does not tell the right
time, it is no use blaming the hands. The trouble lies deeper,   there is something wrong with
the works. (SHOW CLOCK).
The trouble lies inside the clock.   In the part
you can't see.   In the same way your tongue and
mine of course is controlled by something you
can't see; your mind and heart. I think it best
to call it your thoughts. If you ask Jesus to be
your Saviour and live in your heart and thank
Him for dying for you, He will put good thoughts
within you. It will be like giving a watch some
new works.   He will fill your heart with love
for other people and when your heart is full of
love you will find your tongue will only speak
words of kindness. You will find that Jesus has
tamed your tongue." (OPEN BIBLE).
"God has something to say about an untamed tongue," said mother.   "But the tongue can no man
tame.   It is an unruly evil, full of deadly
·poison.".......But with Jesus in your heart your
tongue can be tamed.

     The girls thanked Marion's mother for the
orange drink and chocolate cake but most of all
for her story.
     Betty said, "Every night when I put my head
on my pillow, I shall think of that story, I'll
ask Him into my heart and ask Him to fill me
with good thoughts. We will tell the other girls
the truth about Marion,   fortunately the story
hasn't spread too far yet, at least we will make
sure the girls in our class hear the truth."
     Boys and girls, when you go to bed and put
your head on the pillow you will remember this
story won't you?   Most of all, ask Jesus into
your life to fill your mind with love and good
thoughts.   Then you will never feel the shame
felt by the man with the unruly tongue.

THE HISTORY OF A TREE.

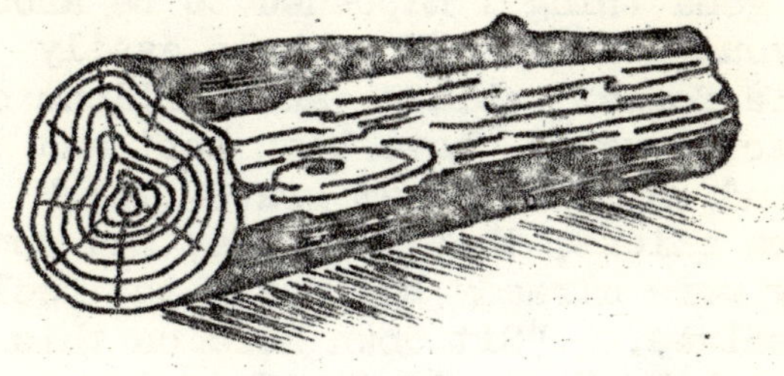

AIM OF LESSON.....Growth in the Christian life.

OBJECTS NEEDED......A section through the trunk or branch of a tree.

> (It is useful to draw a rough sketch of the
> rings on a tree section if you have a large
> number of children present, so that the rings
> can be seen clearly. The heart wood can be
> seen more clearly in some trees than others.
> In your sketch the outer wood could be left
> white and the heart wood coloured orange.).

Alfred and his friend David were spending a day of their holiday wandering through a forest, but after a while they got tired of walking and Alfred suggested it would be good fun to make a fire.   "But on that notice-board over there it says Danger, do not make fires in the forest," replied David.   "No need to take any notice of that, we will just be careful, no-one is looking anyway.   Come on, let's look for sticks," said Alfred crossly.

They were so busy making their fire, that they did not notice a young forester who had walked down the forest glade and who stood silently watching them. Just as Alfred was about to set fire to the sticks, he strode forward and demanded, "What on earth do you think you two are up to?" "Oh! We didn't know you were watching," gasped Alfred, feeling rather frightened. "It's a good thing I happened to be around", went on the young man. "You could easily have set the whole forest ablaze and millions of pounds of property would have been lost and the lives of men and animals put at grave risk." The two boys were silent, they knew they had done wrong, and they were already beginning to feel ashamed of themselves. "Sit down here on this log with me for a while," said the forester. They sat down and Mr. Jackson, for that was his name, picked up a section of a tree trunk which one of the labourers had left lying beside the path.

(SHOW SECTION OF TRUNK TO CHILDREN).

"This is a section cut through a tree - trunk," explained Mr. Jackson. "A tree is a very wonderful plant and you can read its history, not by looking up at it, but by looking at a section through its trunk, like this section here. The tree only shows us its life history after it has been cut down... that is...after it is dead. You will notice that the section is made up of many rings...each circle represents a years growth. There is a small circle right in the centre. Allow four years for that, and then start from there to count the circles until you reach the bark. This tree was about twenty years old."

The forester continued, "A human being resembles a tree. In the first place we cannot tell much by looking at a person. The person

with a very nice outside may be very nasty inside, if you see what I mean."

     David replied, "O yes, that's right, there
is a boy in my class just like that.   Everyone
thinks he is very good looking but we know he is
nothing but a cheat."   "Boys, there is a day
coming when your life and mine will be cut down
....for we too shall die. When that happens God
will read our history as clearly as you can read
the history of this tree, you have counted how
many years it has been growing.   One day God
will reveal just how many years you have served
Him, it doesn't matter how many years you live,
the important thing is how many years have you
served God.   You only begin to live for God the
day you give your life to Jesus.   You can say
then, that the tree of your life started to grow
then.   The Bible says that those who love God
are like trees. They grow to give God pleasure."
(SHOW HEART WOOD).

     "Why is that centre part a darker colour,"
asked David, who was getting really interested.
"This part of the wood is called the heart wood.
It is the most important part of the wood because it is the hardest.   Railway sleepers are
made from this wood.   They carry the enormous
weight of express trains and heavy freight
trucks, no other wood could stand the strain. So
just as the tree has a part of it more important
than any other part,   so there is a part of you
that matters more than anything else, it is your
heart. I don't mean the organ which pumps blood
round your body, I mean the real "YOU." I mean
that inner part of you which feels and thinks
and plans and wishes; Your mind and feelings. If
that part of you has been given to Jesus Christ,
God's Son, and you do all you can to please Him,
to show that you belong to Him, then your heart

is sound.....as sound and as strong as the heart
wood of this tree.   In fact it is even tougher,
for nothing will ever be able to destroy it, you
will live for ever, when your human life is end-
ed.

    Look at this piece of wood.

Notice the rings; at first, the rings are quite
some distance apart,   these are the years when
the tree has made the most growth. Further out ,
towards the bark, the rings are much closer together, then the tree made little growth. Can
you guess why there should be this difference?"
The boys shook their heads. "It was due to competition, when the young trees were planted they
were spaced widely apart,   they each had plenty
of light and nourishment, but the neighbouring
trees, also, began to get bigger. They took up
so much of the light and food that there wasn't
so much left for our tree here,   so its growth
slowed down.

    Just as this tree did well at first, so do
many boys and girls start well, they give their
lives to Jesus and do all they can to please
Him, they feed on God's Word by reading it pray-
erfully each day, but then along comes competition.   They spend far too much time in front of
the television, reading rubbish, or just wasting
time. When they waste their time like that they
are like this tree here,   they make little
growth."

    "Why does a tree have bark," asked Alfred.
"That is there for the tree's protection. Without it, the tree would die. Jesus is our protection,   He helps us to say "No" every time we
are tempted to do wrong things......like making

fires in forests, for instance."

Mr. Jackson smiled at the boys. "Please can I keep this piece of wood?" asked Alfred."It will remind me that my life can be like a tree. I'd like to tell my father all those things you have told us. I'll never think trees don't matter again." Mr. Jackson smiled and handed the wood to Alfred. "Thank you," beamed Alfred. "I don't usually like getting a telling off but I enjoyed the way you did it." Mr. Jackson could not help laughing at this description of his talk. "I used to go to a Bible class where we heard all that sort of thing," said Alfred thoughtfully. "I think I'll start going again." David was thinking much the same thing. "Well, I must be on my way," grinned the forester. "Every time you enjoy trees, remember our little conversation, won't you?" He waved to them as he turned and walked away along the forest path.

A Box Of Long Matches.

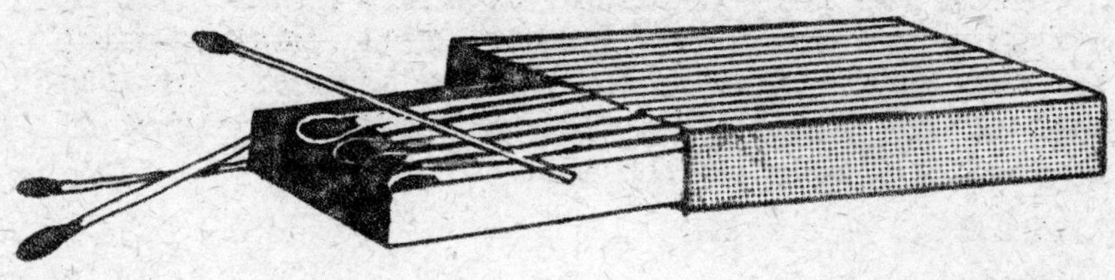

```
AIM OF LESSON.......To show that boys and girls need Jesus and He
                    needs them.
```

```
OBJECTS NEEDED.......A box of long matches or drawing.

                     Words on a large sheet of paper...

                     1. "I NEED JESUS."

                     2. "JESUS NEEDS ME."
```

Jim's Uncle had just returned from Sweden, and he told the boy he had brought him a present. Now Jim had a fine collection of things from all over the world. He called this collection his museum. Jim hoped very much that his Uncle would bring him something specially made in Sweden. He did. This is what be brought him......

(SHOW BOX OF MATCHES).

Can you guess what is in this long box?....yes... matches. They are not like ours, they are very long. Sweden has many large forests and many of the trees are cut down and the wood is turned in- to matches. These matches are sent all over the world. Of course most of them are ordinary small matches such as we use here, but these giant mat-

ches are used for the tourists to take back with
them.   You can also buy them in Britain in some
of the larger stores.

        Jim was very pleased with his giant box of
matches, he could hardly wait till next morning
to take them to school to show teacher and the
rest of the class. He took one out and struck it
against the side of the box.

(STRIKE ONE OF THE MATCHES).

He had never seen such a huge match and it burnt
for a very long time.   Then he went up to his
room and put the box with the rest of his treas-
ures.

        That night he had a strange dream; he dream-
ed that the box opened all by itself.

(SLOWLY OPEN BOX).

Then three of the matches jumped out and began to
talk to one another, the first said,   "It's easy
to see why I am in this fine box."

(TAKE OUT THREE MATCHES AS YOU TALK).

He continued,   "I am larger than any of you and
when I'm struck I shall have a longer life than
any of you.   I shall have a long useful life, in
fact I think I am the most important match in the
box." The second match said, "What rubbish. I'm
the most important.   Can't you see I'm made of
far better quality wood than the rest of you. The
rest of you will probably end up as a bundle of
splinters, you are made of such common stuff.When
I am lit I shall stand firm and straight."   The
third match laughed, "I never heard such boast-
ings. ANYONE can see I'm the most important.I've
got a bigger head than the rest of you and it's
the best head that counts in this life.   Think
what a fine blaze I shall make when I'm struck,

I'll be as good as a firework."   So the three
matches went on quarreling, their voices rising
higher and higher with pride and anger. Then Jim
heard a low gruff voice, it was the box speaking!
It said, "Listen you foolish fellows, can any one
of you light yourself? Of course you can't. You
are of no use to anyone without me.   You depend
on me alone to give any light at all."

        Just then, Jim woke up.   What a strange
dream he had had!   It was so strange, that Jim
sat up in bed, clasped his arms around his knees
and had a good long think about it. Where had he
heard talk very like this before? Then he remembered!   It was in Sunday School, Mr. Wright, his
teacher had been telling them that unless his
boys gave their lives to Jesus, they would be of
no real use to anyone.   You can't fight sin on
your own," he said.   "You need Jesus, with His
help you can be truthful, honest, brave, kind and
hard working.   You cannot go to Heaven on your
own. You need Jesus to take you there. You cannot find true lasting happiness on your own. You
need the joy that Jesus can give you. You cannot
make a success of life on your own, You need
Jesus to guide you."

(SHOW THE WORDS "I NEED JESUS").

        All that Jim's teacher said is true, boys
and girls, but there is something I should like
to add to that. While it is true to say that the
matches must have the box to be of any use, it is
also true to say that the box needs the matches.
You need Jesus, Jesus needs you.

(SHOW THE WORDS "JESUS NEEDS YOU").

Jesus is God's son and he could have arranged
life so that he had no need of you, but you see,
He doesn't want to do that. Your Mummy and Daddy
could live without you, but they don't want to do

that. They prefer to have you around, they WANT
you to be part of their family and to play your
part in that family. If you belong to Jesus, you
are part of God's family, and he has work for you
to do. There is a hymn which says, quite rightly
....."There's a work for Jesus only you can do."
Perhaps there is not another Christian in your
class? You could invite some of your class to
Sunday School or to Sunshine Corner or to your
"Good News Club."   Perhaps an old person in your
street has no one to run errands for him.   You
may be the only boy in the street who knows his
need.   Perhaps your mother is very, very tired
and you are the only one in the family who can
take the baby and play with it and give mother a
rest...that's a work for Jesus only you can do.

        So, every time you see a box of matches, stop
and think...
(SHOW THE WORDS..."I NEED JESUS"
                "JESUS NEEDS ME").

✱ CRABS ✱

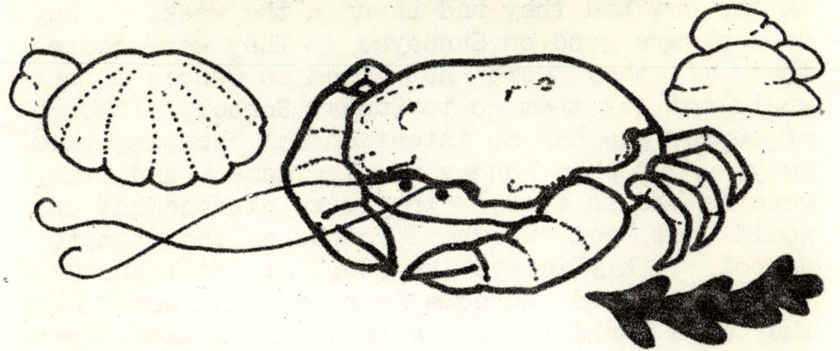

AIM OF LESSON.....To show the children it is not enough to be good
                only on Sundays or special occasions and that
                only those who belong to Jesus can have victory
                over sin.

OBJECTS NEEDED.....A crab (or picture of one.).

    Harry and Elizabeth were twins,   they were
always getting into mischief.   Mummy and Daddy
thought they were old enough to start Sunday
School, so they took them along. The "terrible
twins", as Daddy called them, were soon enrolled
in a class.

    Harry and Elizabeth loved Sunday School.
Their teacher was very good to them and sometimes,   after she had told them a story, she
would set out a very large tray, filled with
sand.   The twins and the other children would
take some little dolls or tin soldiers or animals,   and would act out the story they had just

heard.   Harry would heap up the sand to form
mountains and Elizabeth would make a long twisty
line in the sand and pretend it was a river.They
could hardly wait for next Sunday to come,   no
matter how bad they had been in the week,   they
were always good on Sundays.   They were scared
that if they were not good on Sunday mother
would not let them go to Sunday School, although
of course she had no intention of keeping them
away.   But when Monday morning came round, they
were as bad as ever,   they were disobedient and
would not get up when mother called them for
school.   They teased the poor cat until she was
too frightened to come near them and sometimes
they even told lies,   a thing which made their
parents very sad,   but they did none of these
things on Sundays,   they always kept their best
clothes and their best behaviour for Sundays.

One day, Daddy and the twins were having a
walk along by the sea-side.   Suddenly Harry saw
a dead crab and he gave it to his Daddy to look
at.   It was something like this one...

(HOLD UP CRAB).

Now you all know that crabs can nip your
toes if you are not careful, but there is something else, very strange about a crab. As far
as I know,   it is the only creature which walks
sideways.   Try if for yourselves sometimes!
Daddy began to talk to the twins about how the
crabs walk sideways, instead of going straight,
then he told them a story, of course it isn't a
true story, but it is a story with a meaning:-

One day, a great big cod and some of his
friends happened to notice that all the crabs
walked sideways. "This is very serious,"exclaimed the great cod.   "All other creatures go
straight ahead,   we must start a Sunday School

for young crabs and we will teach them to walk
straight."   So a Sunday School was started and
all the young crabs came along. They had a wonderful time, marching up and down on the sea-bed
doing right turns and left turns, and at the end
of the very first Sunday, those crabs could walk
straight.   The great cod fish was delighted and
he told them all to keep practising and to come
back next Sunday so that he could see how well
they were doing.   Next Sunday came and all the
young crabs came back to Sunday School,   but
dear me, they all came walking sideways!   The
great cod was very patient and once more he
taught them all to walk straight, but the next
week the same thing happened..all the crabs came
into school walking sideways. This went on week
after week until even kind, patient Mr. Cod gave
up. Do you know what he said to those silly,
young crabs,   "It's no use walking straight on
Sundays if you walk sideways all the rest of the
week."

        Poor Mr. Cod, he had to give up, didn't he?
He couldn't really help those young crabs, but
the twins were better off than the crabs because
they had their Daddy to help them.

        Boys and girls,   there is Someone who can
help you be good every day of the week and every
minute of the day,   that Person is Jesus.   Ask
Him to be your Saviour and friend.   Just say to
Him when you pray, "Lord Jesus, I give you my
life, because you gave your life for me upon the
cruel cross,help me to be good like you. Help me
to be good every day of the week. Help me always
to walk straight."

Precious...but unseen.

(THE DISCOVERY OF RADIUM)

AIM OF LESSON.......To show the reality of the unseen Jesus.

OBJECTS NEEDED.....1.   Drawing of a cross.

2.   Words on large sheets of paper as follows:-

"UNSEEN"

NO-ONE BELIEVED

RADIUM

JESUS CHRIST IS MY GREATEST DISCOVERY

SIN

3.   Sketch of a black heart and a white heart.

Many years ago, but within living memory, there lived a very clever man with an equally brilliant wife. They were both scientists, their names were Pierre and Marie Curie, they lived in Paris and studied at the famous Sorbonne University.

They made the discovery that common pitch-

blende ores threw out some very mysterious rays
which had never been known before. They couldn't
think what caused these mysterious rays, it could
not be the dirty pitchblende, they must be caused by some other substance hidden somewhere in
the ore. They talked a lot about this substance
which caused the mysterious rays, but even clever
scientists said at first, "How can you expect us
to believe that there is something hidden away in
the pitchblende?" We cannot see it or find any
other evidence that it is there."

(SHOW THE WORD "UNSEEN").

You see, children, because nothing could be
seen it could not be believed by most people.
Some people say this kind of thing about God
although they can see all the wonderful things He
has made, they say they cannot believe He exists
because they cannot <u>see</u> Him.

Marie and Pierre were not stopped by the
foolish talk of other people.   "We believe that
this mysterious substance which gives off these
rays is hidden away in the pitchblende and we in-
tend to separate this substance from the ore. "
These were brave words because they did not know
that for every-ton of pitchblende there was only
a grain of this unknown substance.

At last they decided to buy tons and tons of
pitchblende and heat it until it became so hot it
would melt. They would then in some way pour off
the pitchblende and be left with the hidden substance. They asked the university for a splendid
modern laboratory in which to carry out their
experiments, but no one believed in what they
were trying to do.

(SHOW WORDS "NO-ONE BELIEVED").

All they could get was an old leaky shed, and a
huge metal boiler. They set to work, Marie sometimes passed a whole day stirring a boiling mass
of molten mineral with a metal rod, nearly as big
as herself, by evening she felt ill with tired-
ness, yet she was so convinced that the hidden
substance was there to be discovered.   Later she
said that those years of toil were the happiest
she ever spent in her life.

   Pierre wanted to give up but Marie said she
would go on no matter what happened.   Often she
was tired and wet and racked with coughing and
pain, yet she was so sure of finding that which
was hidden she would not give up.
   At last, after four years of extremely difficult work, a tiny amount of the hidden substance
was found.   Marie had been right.   One evening
Pierre and Marie came into the shed and noticed
the mysterious substance they had discovered,
shining in the darkness.· They were so thrilled
by its unexpected beauty that they gave it the
name "RADIUM".

(SHOW THE WORD "RADIUM").

They named it after the word radiance on account
of its beauty. It is almost the same word, isn't
it?

   The two scientists became famous all over
the world, because they had proved the existence
of a substance no one else had the brains or
courage to believe in.   What is more they had
proved that what was unseen could, by searching,
be found and that it was beautiful and wonderful.

   When Jesus came into this world, He came for
one thing, to show us what God is really like.
Before Jesus came, the people who lived in Old
Testament times knew there was a God, because of

all the wonderful things He had made in the world around them, but they could not <u>find</u> Him. He was hidden. Jesus was not only a man, He was the Son of God.   By His spotless life and by rising from the dead, He proved that the hidden God had been seen and heard, in and through Him.

One famous scientist was once asked which of his discoveries he considered the greatest. This is what he said......

(SHOW WORDS "JESUS CHRIST IS MY GREATEST DISCOVERY").

Will you please all read out loud what he said... After He rose from the dead, Jesus went back into Heaven once more.   At present He is hidden, but for over thirty three years, He could be seen and heard and known. His disciples <u>saw</u> Him go back into Heaven, they knew He was still alive. Even though Jesus is still hidden it is possible for boys and girls to be sure that He is alive. When we invite Him into our hearts, He comes and gives us victory over Satan. When we ask Him for things in prayer, He answers our prayers.

(SHOW THE WORD "RADIUM").

Like the unseen radium which was present all the time, Jesus is real to us and we can know Him even better than our best friend.   When the Curie's first discovered radium they had no idea how precious it would turn out to be.   It can sometimes be used in the curing of a terrible disease called cancer. It is more precious to us than gold.   However, boys and girls, there is a disease far deadlier than cancer.   Sin destroys body, mind and spirit. It shuts us out of Heaven if we do not get rid of it.

(SHOW THE WORD "SIN").

Only the precious radium can cure cancer and it takes something precious to cure us of our

sinning and cleanse our hearts from sin's stain.
It is something which <u>was</u> seen nearly 2,000 years
ago, but which no one can see today.   It is the
precious blood which Jesus shed when He died upon
the cross.

(SHOW CROSS).

<u>We</u> should have been punished for our own sin, but
Jesus took our place.   On the cross, He has already died for our sin so God will not punish us,
as well, if we will only thank Jesus and invite
Him into our lives and live to please Him.   The
moment a boy or girl asks Him to forgive their
.sin and allows Him into their lives, they can say,
"The precious blood of Jesus cleanses me from all
sin." Our black hearts become so white that when
we die, Jesus will welcome us into Heaven.

(SHOW SKETCH OF BLACK HEART AND THEN WHITE HEART).

How can we ask Jesus into our lives - The
words are very simple. They are....."Lord Jesus,
I am sorry for my sins.   Thank you for dying a
cruel death for me.   I love you because of what
you have done for me. Please take my black heart
and make it white.   Come and live in my heart."
If you really mean these words He will answer
that prayer and the unseen God will come to dwell
with you and be in you for always.

Moorley's Bible & Bookshop Ltd. are
growing publishers adding several new
titles each year. We specialise in books
of :-

    Recitations for children
    Verse for Women's meetings, etc.
    Books of Prayers
    Religious Monologues etc. for adult use
    Plays for children, teenagers and adults
    Sunday School Anniversary Demonstrations

****

Please write for current list or
consult your Christian Bookseller who should
carry all our titles.

****